TABLE OF CONTENTS

D1311401

Unless otherwise indicated, all Scripture quotations are taken from the King James Version of the Bible.
Creating Tomorrow Through Seed-Faith
ISBN 10: 1-56394-022-1/ISBN 13: 978-1563940224/B-06
Copyright © 2003 by **MIKE MURDOCK**
All publishing rights belong exclusively to Wisdom International
Publisher/Editor: Deborah Murdock Johnson
Published by The Wisdom Center · 4051 Denton Hwy. · Ft. Worth, Texas 76117
1-817-759-BOOK · 1-817-759-2665 · 1-817-759-0300
You Will Love Our Website..! WisdomOnline.com

If God Is Holding Your Seed,
Today Is The Poorest
You Will Ever Be.

-MIKE MURDOCK

≈ 1 ≈

GOD IS YOUR TOTAL SOURCE FOR EVERY GOOD THING YOU WANT TO HAPPEN IN YOUR LIFE

God Is The Master Giver.

"Every good gift and every perfect gift is from above, and cometh down from the Father of lights, with Whom is no variableness, neither shadow of turning," (James 1:17).

Your loved ones may often become His channels, but He is the true source. Your boss and company officials may be favorable and generous to you, but He is the cause and source. This is so important. Otherwise, you will become bitter and resentful of any person who slows your progress or "robs" you of a success.

"For promotion cometh neither from the east, nor from the west, nor from the south. But God is the judge: He putteth down one, and setteth up another," (Psalm 75:6-7).

Nobody is more misunderstood than God.

Many believe that God is simply a spiritual force, a supreme being, "the Man upstairs."

They have not fully understood that He is "touched with the feeling of our infirmities," (Hebrews 4:15).

God invited us to approach Him boldly for every need in our life. "Let us therefore come boldly unto the throne of grace, that we may obtain mercy, and find grace to help in time of need," (Hebrews 4:16). Obviously, *you* must have the *sensitivity* to know *when* you need Him, the *humility* to pursue His mercy, and the *desperation* to come boldly to Him.

Someone once said that twenty percent of what Jesus talked about involved finances. He cared.

8 Reasons God Wants You To Prosper

1. God Wants You To Have Enough Finances To Provide Everything Your Loved Ones Need For Their Success. "But if any provide not for his own, and specially for those of his own house, he hath denied the faith, and is worse than an infidel," (1 Timothy 5:8).

2. God Wants You To Have Enough Finances To Provide An Uncommon And Wonderful Income For Your Spiritual Leaders And Pastors. "Let the elders that rule well be counted worthy of double honour, especially they who labour in the word and doctrine. For the scripture saith, Thou shalt not muzzle the ox that treadeth out the corn. And, The labourer is worthy of his reward," (1 Timothy 5:17-18).

3. God Wants You To Have Enough Finances To Send Ministers Throughout The World Preaching The Gospel. "And how shall they preach, except they be sent? as it is written, How beautiful are the feet of them that preach the gospel of peace, and bring glad tidings of good things!" (Romans 10:15).

4. God Wants To Provide Enough

Finances For You To Pay Your Taxes And Obligations. "Render therefore unto Caesar the things which are Caesar's; and unto God the things that are God's," (Matthew 22:21).

5. **God Wants You To Have Enough Finances To Return The Tithe Back To His House That Belongs To The Work of God.** "And all the tithe of the land, whether of the Seed of the land, or of the fruit of the tree, is the Lord's: it is holy unto the Lord," (Leviticus 27:30).

6. **God Wants You To Have Enough Finances To Give Good And Uncommon Gifts To Your Children And Those You Love.** "If ye then, being evil, know how to give good gifts unto your children, how much more shall your Father which is in Heaven give good things to them that ask Him?" (Matthew 7:11).

7. **God Wants You To Have Enough Finances To Help The Poor.** "He that hath pity upon the poor lendeth unto the Lord; and that which he hath given will He pay him again," (Proverbs 19:17).

8. **God Wants You To Have Enough Money To Solve Any Emergency Problem Or Crisis That Arises.** "Money answereth all things," (Ecclesiastes 10:19).

10 Facts God Wants You To Know About Money

1. **God Wants To Reveal To You Where Your Financial Provisions Are Located.** He proved this to Elijah. "Turn thee eastward, and hide thyself by the brook Cherith, that is before Jordan...I

have commanded the ravens to feed thee there," (1 Kings 17:3-4).

2.   God Is Concerned Every Time You Have A Financial Crisis And Will Give You Instructions To Turn It Around. He did it for Elijah. "And it came to pass after a while, that the brook dried up, because there had been no rain in the land. And the word of the Lord came unto him, saying, Arise, get thee to Zarephath, which belongeth to Zidon, and dwell there," (1 Kings 17:7-9).

3.   God Will Give People Instructions To Help You In Financial Crisis. Again, He did it for the prophet Elijah, and He will do it for you! "Arise, get thee to Zarephath, which belongeth to Zidon, and dwell there: behold, I have commanded a widow woman there to sustain thee," (1 Kings 17:9).

4.   God Always Rewards Holy Conduct And Behavior With Financial Provision. "...No good thing will He withhold from them that walk uprightly," (Psalm 84:11).

5.   God Commanded Everything He Created To Multiply And Become More. "And God said, Let the earth bring forth grass, the herb yielding Seed, and the fruit tree yielding fruit after his kind, whose Seed is in itself, upon the earth...Let the waters bring forth abundantly the moving creature that hath life, and fowl that may fly above the earth...Be fruitful, and multiply, and fill the waters in the seas, and let fowl multiply in the earth," (Genesis 1:11, 20, 22).

6.   God Commanded People To Multiply And Become More. "Be fruitful, and multiply, and replenish the earth, and subdue it: and have dominion over the fish of the sea, and over the fowl of the air, and over every living thing that moveth upon the earth," (Genesis 1:28).

7. God Even Rewards Productivity With More Increase. Read the incredible story of the talents in Matthew 25. "Well done, good and faithful servant; thou hast been faithful over a few things, I will make thee ruler over many things: enter thou into the joy of thy lord," (Matthew 25:23).

8. God Punishes Those Who Refuse To Use Their Gifts And Talents To Become More. "Take therefore the talent from him, and give it unto him which hath ten talents...cast ye the unprofitable servant into outer darkness: there shall be weeping and gnashing of teeth," (Matthew 25:28, 30).

9. God Always Promises Financial Blessing To Those Obedient To His Instructions, Laws And Principles. "...If thou shalt hearken diligently unto the voice of the Lord thy God, to observe and to do all His commandments which I command thee this day...all these blessings shall come on thee, and overtake thee...The Lord shall command the blessing upon thee in thy storehouses...And the Lord shall make thee plenteous in goods...The Lord shall open unto thee His good treasure, the Heaven to give the rain unto thy land in His season, and to bless all the work of thine hand: and thou shalt lend unto many nations, and thou shalt not borrow," (Deuteronomy 28:1-2, 8, 11-12).

10. God Will Teach You To Profit, Through Mentors, The Holy Spirit And His Word. "Thus saith the Lord, thy redeemer, the Holy One of Israel; I am the Lord thy God which teacheth thee to profit, which leadeth thee by the way that thou shouldest go," (Isaiah 48:17).

So, become excited about your financial future.

Anything God Touches Multiplies.

-MIKE MURDOCK

❦ 2 ❦

YOUR LIFE IS A COLLECTION OF HARVESTS YOU HAVE ALREADY RECEIVED FROM GOD

You Are Already Prospering.

You Have Already Received Harvests From God.

Your talents...energy...friendships...finances...ideas... blessings of every kind...are *gifts* from God.

"...and what hast thou that thou didst not receive? now if thou didst receive it, why dost thou glory, as if thou hadst not received it?" (1 Corinthians 4:7).

Harvests occur daily in your life.

What is a Harvest? A Harvest is *any good thing God sends into your life.*

A Harvest is *any person* who blesses, encourages, corrects, strengthens or improves you.

A Harvest is *any idea* planted by your Creator that has potential for helping others.

A Harvest is *any opportunity* to increase your finances, maximize your standard of excellence or unlock a gift or skill within you. It is any opportunity you have to solve a problem.

Almost nobody recognizes a Harvest when it occurs.

Your life has been a parade of Harvests. See, you must learn to *recognize* your Harvest. Your

Harvest is *any person or anything that can bless or benefit you.* It may be someone who can contribute something you need—information, favor, finances, an explosive idea or encouragement when you need it most. A Harvest is when somebody recommends you to another person. This creates the flow of favor and acceptance toward your life. *Access to someone who believes in you is a Harvest.*

Your Harvest already exists.

It is walking around you! Just as your eyes had to be opened to recognize Jesus, your eyes also must be opened to *recognize your Harvests* as they come. The entire world missed the *Harvest of Jesus.* "He was in the world, and the world was made by Him, and the world knew Him not. He came unto His own, and His own received Him not," (John 1:10-11). How tragic! Spiritual leaders, such as the Pharisees, failed to recognize Him! Politicians of His day *failed to see Him as their Harvest.*

What do you have that God did not give you?

It is He that keeps breathing His breath into you. You could not breathe another minute if God did not breathe into you.

You could not walk another step *if God were not there.*

You could not live another day *if His presence were withheld from you.*

Everything you possess came from Him.

Everything you will ever own in your future must come from God.

Our Prayer Together...

"Father, forgive us for ingratitude, unthankfulness and *any blindness toward the Harvest* You have provided. It is true that our complaining spirit has robbed us and aborted many miracles You had scheduled for us. In the name of Jesus, I release myself to You. I give all of me to You, knowing that You will reveal wonderful and powerful things to me. Thank You for my *health,* my *eyesight* and *ability to walk* today. Thank You for the mind that You have given me, and the *doors of favor* that have opened into my life. You are a marvelous, powerful and giving God. *I am thankful.* I am grateful. And I shall not forget Your hand of blessing in my life. Show me what to do. I will obey You. I will listen to Your voice, and I will be swift to give You the glory and praise for every good thing You do for me. You will receive ten percent of everything You bless me with, and even more as You provide. I *thank You* for every blessing in the name of Jesus. Amen."

Your Rewards In Life Are
Determined By
The Kind of Problems
You Are Willing
To Solve For Others.

-MIKE MURDOCK

∾ 3 ∾

A SEED IS ANYTHING YOU CAN DO THAT CAN HELP ANOTHER PERSON

Everything You Have Can Be A Seed.

A Seed is a tiny beginning with a huge future. It is anything that can *become more.* It is the *Beginning.* It is anything you can *do, know* or *possess* that can improve the life of another.

Your *Thoughts* are Seeds for desired behavior, conduct and creativity.

Your *Love* is a Seed for relationships.

Your *Time* is a Seed.

Your *Patience* is a Seed.

Your *Money* is a Seed.

Your *Kindness* is a Seed to others.

Your *Prayers* are Seeds.

Stopping slander is a Seed.

Thankfulness is a Seed.

Your Seed is anything you have received from God that can be traded for something else.

You are a walking warehouse of Seeds. Most people do not even know this. They have no idea how many Seeds they contain that can be planted into the lives of others.

▶ Anything that improves another is a *Seed.*

▶ Anything that makes another smile is a *Seed.*

▶ Anything that makes someone's life easier *is a Seed.*

It is more important to inventory your own Seeds. Stop focusing on what you *do not* have, and look closer at something you *already have been given.*

Something you have been given will create anything else you have been promised.

Little things birth big things. Acorns become oak trees.

Showing up at work *on time*...is a Seed.

Showing up *ahead of time* is another Seed. You see, anything that you can do to make life easier for your boss or anyone else...is a Seed.

Millions have never used ten percent of the Seed stored within them. You see, mowing the grass for your church is a Seed. Baby-sitting for a struggling single parent is a Seed.

You are a living collection of Seeds, a warehouse of powerful, tiny golden passionate *beginnings.*

You must recognize the Seeds God has already stored within you. Your Seed is any gift, skill, or talent that God has provided for you to sow into the lives of others around you. Do not hide it.

Use your Seed. Celebrate the existence of Seeds in your life...that are carving the road to your future. Even Joseph recognized his ability to interpret dreams. He wanted to help others. When Pharaoh became troubled, Joseph had a Seed to sow toward his life. "A man's gift maketh room for him, and bringeth him before great men," (Proverbs 18:16).

You need somebody to help you sow the Seed you already possess. You need someone to show you a picture of the future within it.

Develop an appreciation for the man of God who helps you *discover your Seed,* and provides a photograph of the Harvest *you can expect.*

Elijah did it. It turned a poor woman into a miracle woman. From poverty to plenty. From famine to supply.

Look, look and look again for opportunities to plant a Seed. They surround you every day. *Hundreds of them.*

Every Seed is a Golden Door from your present into your future.

If you do not recognize a Seed, how could you ever recognize the Harvest from it?

If a farmer has never seen what a kernel of corn looks like, do you think he would recognize a field of stalks of corn on the side of the road? Of course not. You cannot begin to recognize a Harvest until you recognize a Seed—something precious within you God has enabled you to *know, do* or *possess* and sow.

You are a Walking Warehouse of Seeds. Invest Time in The Secret Place—your personal place of prayer. **Ask The Holy Spirit to show you what you have been given, supernaturally and naturally to plant into the lives of others.** Your future is in your own hands.

▶ You can *see something* nobody else can see.
▶ You already *know something* others do not know.
▶ You can *solve problems* others cannot solve. Solving them is your Seed that brings any kind of Harvest you desire.

Millions have no idea what a Seed really is, so they never receive the Harvest from it because it goes unplanted and unsown.

Discover the Seeds you have already received from God and your future can be anything you desire.

Any act of kindness...your prayer for a sick loved

one...a thoughtful word of encouragement...your tithes and offerings to the work of God...anything that you do or say that could help someone is a Seed. In fact, you are a Seed.

We are encouraged to sow good Seeds into the lives of others.

"Withhold not good from them to whom it is due, when it is in the power of thine hand to do it," (Proverbs 3:27).

"As we have therefore opportunity, let us do good unto all men, especially unto them who are of the household of faith," (Galatians 6:10).

Somebody needs you today. Perhaps you know a small bit of information that is vital to their success. Will you share it? That is your Seed in their lives. When a ministry asks you for financial assistance on a project, that is your Seed. Does your boss need you to go the "extra mile?" Plant it as a Seed unto the Lord.

"Servants, be obedient to them that are your masters according to the flesh...With good will doing service, as to the Lord, and not to men: Knowing that whatsoever good thing any man doeth, the same shall he receive of the Lord," (Ephesians 6:5, 7-8).

In fact, attentiveness to the unique needs of your mate can produce miraculous results. That is sowing good Seeds!

Your Seed may leave your hand, but it will never leave your life. When you sow it, it exits your present state, but enters your future where it begins to multiply.

Years ago my son was very worried over some of his grades in school. His voice was breaking, "Dad, math is hard for me. I'm just not doing good in math. I just can't seem to catch on."

I explained to my son how the good things of life sometimes take us a little longer to obtain. A little more sacrifice. I talked about friendships being built stronger through hours spent together; how experts become knowledgeable when they devote their time and total attention to discovering the secrets of whatever special topic they are studying.

I reminded him that greatness costs...but, the rewards are well worth the price. I encouraged him to *invest some extra time* in private talks with his teacher...to give total focus and attention each evening to his math...those hours were like Seeds—producing knowledge, high marks and lifetime benefits.

You see, I really explained the Law of Seed-Faith. He could *create* the grades he wanted—by *sowing* his *time.*

What God Has Already Given To You Is Enough To Create What He Has Not Yet Given To You.

What you have is a Seed; what God has is a Harvest. You sow your Seed...in faith that God will honor it by returning to you the desired Harvest.

Tomorrow can be anything you want it to be—a tomorrow filled with happiness, good health, spiritual power, financial freedom, a vibrant marriage...anything. That's what Seed-Faith is all about; *Creating The Future You Desire...*by trusting God enough to sow your Seeds of love, time and finances *back into His world* for a desired Harvest.

When you sow wrong Seeds, you stain the future with heartache.

When you sow good Seeds, you unleash a thousand miracles. "For he that soweth to his flesh shall of the flesh reap corruption; but he that soweth to the Spirit shall of the Spirit reap life everlasting," (Galatians 6:8).

Let me say something to you, too, my dear friend. God sees you, also.

God knows where you hurt the most. He knows who has stripped you of your joy, your victory, your possessions.

God is not through blessing you today. Tomorrow is not here yet. You can still make it *anything* you want it to be.

Elijah was a Seed-Faith prophet. He saw *more* than her Seed—he saw the Harvest it could produce. He mentored her about her receiving a Divine, supernatural Harvest.

She did not argue that she "deserved to die." She did not quarrel over the "theology of it." She did not whine that it sounded "selfish and greedy."

She wanted to LIVE. I am sure that she despised poverty and hated her circumstances of lack. She knew that she had to change her belief system before she could change what was happening in her life. She had several characteristics of a winner: The ability to recognize a man of God when she saw him, the willingness to listen to the Wisdom of his instructions, and the faith to sow a tomorrow of blessings into visibility.

Her key to her future was in her hand. She discovered that you always have enough to create what you do not have.

You, too, can write a new page in your life. You can create any tomorrow you need.

You already have in your hand everything it takes to make tomorrow what it should be.

This is the most powerful master key I have ever discovered. You, too, can use it to unlock the door to the miracles you are needing in your life today.

Now begin to look for ways to put the Seed-Faith principle to work in your life, your family, your job and the work of God. Start expecting extraordinary blessings to happen for you. Your Harvest is closer than you may realize. When your Seed leaves your hand, a Harvest will leave the warehouses of Heaven toward you!

My dear friend, Richard Roberts, sings a song that I wrote several years ago called, "I Started Living When I Started Giving To God."

I STARTED LIVING WHEN I STARTED GIVING TO GOD

There are pages of life
I truly regret
Lost everything I had
Stayed deep in debt
Then one day I happened to read
In Malachi chapter three
That my release would bring an increase for me

I started living when I started giving to God
I started living when I started giving to God
Pressed down, shaken together,
Running over, He's blessing me
I started living when I started giving to God
Soon I had some friends
Who had to criticize
Would not receive what I believed
They failed to realize
Jesus said, "If you plant a Seed,
I'm going to make it grow"
2 Corinthians nine, verse six—you're going
    to reap
From every Seed you sow.

My dear partner, something good is being scheduled for your life! Sow with joy and faith in a Divine Harvest. You are creating tomorrow...TODAY.

Everything You Possess Is
Your Seed Or
Your Harvest.

-MIKE MURDOCK

≈ 5 ≈

55 FACTS ABOUT SEED-SOWING

1. Seed-Faith Is The Principle That You Can Produce Anything You Want In Your Future From Something You Are Holding Today.
2. Seed-Faith Is Sowing What You Have Been Given To Create What You Have Been Promised.
3. Your Seed Is Anything That Blesses Somebody.
4. Your Seed Is Any Tool God Has Given You To Create Your Future.
5. God Always Gives You Something To Begin Your Future.
6. There Will Never Be A Day In Your Life That You Have Nothing To Sow.
7. The Instruction You Follow Determines The Future You Create.
8. Something You Have Been Given By God Will Create Anything Else You Have Ever Been Promised By God.
9. Every Seed Contains A Billion, Tiny, Golden, Passionate Beginnings of Miracles.
10. Something You Already Possess Is Your Key To Your Future.
11. When You Let Go of What Is In Your Hand, God Will Let Go of What Is In His Hand.
12. When You Keep What Is In Your Hand, God Will Keep What Is In His Hand.

13. **If You Keep What You Presently Have, That Is The Most It Will Ever Be.**
14. **Everything Within You Is A Seed Someone Has Sown Into You, With Or Without Your Permission.**
15. **Your Seed Is Something Little That Can Become Huge Tomorrow.**
16. **Your Seed Is The Only Proof You Have Mastered Greed.**
17. **Some Seed In Your Present Will Soon Explode Into Something Magnificent In Your Future.**
18. **When You Increase The Size of Your Seed, You Increase The Size of Your Harvest.**
19. **A Seed of Nothing Guarantees A Season of Nothing.**
20. **Your Seed Must Be Comparable To The Harvest You Are Desiring.**
21. **Your Seed Will Shorten The Season of Now.**
22. **When You Get Involved With God's Dream, He Will Get Involved With Your Dream.**
23. **Nobody Can Stop The Harvest Your Seed Has Commanded.**
24. **Every Seed Contains An Invisible Instruction.**
25. **When You Give Your Seed A Specific Assignment, Incredible Faith Is Unleashed.**
26. **Your Seed Is Always The Door Out of Trouble.**
27. **Any Step Towards Self-Sufficiency Is A Step Away From God.**
28. **Your Seed Is The Only Proof of Expectation.**
29. **You Are Never Closer To God Than When**

You Sow A Seed Inspired By A Man of God.

30. Sow That Which Is Eternal, And You Will Create An Eternal Bond of Loyalty With Others.

31. Your Seed Is The Vehicle Into Your Future.

32. Your Seed Is The Only Influence You Have Over Your Future.

33. Your Seed Is A Weapon Against Greed, Fear And Unbelief.

34. Your Seed Forces The Future To Whimper At Your Feet Like A Puppy, Begging For An Instruction.

35. The Seed of Forgiveness Unleashes One Thousand Times More Mercy Back To You.

36. The Seed of Love Creates The Harvest of Love Around You.

37. The Seed of Excellence Creates The Harvest of Excellence Around You.

38. The Seed of Diligence Will Create The Harvest of Access To Leaders.

39. The Seed of Favor Creates The Harvest of Favor Toward You.

40. What You Are Talking About The Most Is Revealing What You Are Expecting In Your Life.

41. What You Are Talking About The Most Is Beginning To Increase In Your Life.

42. Expect The Impossible And The Impossible Will Move Quickly Toward You.

43. The Seed That Would Leave Your Hand Would Never Leave Your Life—Just Your Hand, And Enter Into Your Future Where It Would Multiply!

44. When God Talks To You About A Seed, He Has A Harvest On His Mind.
45. An Uncommon Seed Always Creates An Uncommon Harvest.
46. Everything You Possess Is Something You Have Been Given.
47. Your Seed Is The Only Master Your Future Will Obey.
48. The Seed of Forgiveness Into Others Creates The Harvest of Mercy From Others.
49. What You Keep Is Your Harvest; What You Sow Is Your Seed.
50. When God Talks To You About A Seed, He Has A Harvest On His Mind.
51. When You Sow Into Others What Nobody Else Is Willing To Sow, You Will Reap What No One Else Has Ever Reaped.
52. Your Seed Is A Photograph of Your Faith.
53. Nothing Leaves Heaven Until Something Leaves Earth.
54. When You Ask God For A Harvest, God Will Always Ask You For A Seed.
55. Your Seed Is What God Multiplies; Your Faith Is Why He Multiplies It.

DECISION

Will You Accept Jesus As Your Personal Savior Today?

The Bible says, "That if thou shalt confess with thy mouth the Lord Jesus, and shalt believe in thine heart that God hath raised Him from the dead, thou shalt be saved," (Romans 10:9).

Pray this prayer from your heart today!

"Dear Jesus, I believe that You died for me and rose again on the third day. I confess I am a sinner...I need Your love and forgiveness...Come into my heart. Forgive my sins. I receive Your eternal life. Confirm Your love by giving me peace, joy and supernatural love for others. Amen."

DR. MIKE MURDOCK

is in tremendous demand as one of the most dynamic speakers in America today.

More than 17,000 audiences in over 100 countries have attended his Schools of Wisdom and conferences. Hundreds of invitations come to him from churches, colleges and business corporations. He is a noted author of over 250 books, including the best sellers, *The Leadership Secrets of Jesus* and *Secrets of the Richest Man Who Ever Lived.* Thousands view his weekly television program, *Wisdom Keys with Mike Murdock.* Many attend his Schools of Wisdom that he hosts in many cities of America.

Clip and Mail

☐ Yes, Mike, I made a decision to accept Christ as my personal Savior today. Please send me my free gift of your book, *31 Keys to a New Beginning* to help me with my new life in Christ.

NAME   BIRTHDAY

ADDRESS

CITY   STATE   ZIP

PHONE   E-MAIL   DFC

Mail to: **The Wisdom Center** · 4051 Denton Hwy. · Ft. Worth, TX 76117
1-817-759-BOOK · 1-817-759-2665 · 1-817-759-0300
You Will Love Our Website..! WisdomOnline.com   27

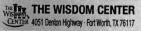

CPSIA information can be obtained at www.ICGtesting.com
Printed in the USA
LVOW050210050113

314373LV00003B/169/P